Tola'at Shani - The Crimson Worm of Psalm 22

Jesus in the Old Testament

George Crabb

Published by The Whole Bible with George Crabb, 2021.

TOLA'AT SHANI - THE CRIMSON WORM OF PSALM 22

First edition. February 15, 2021.

Copyright © 2021 George Crabb.

ISBN: 979-8227939630

Written by George Crabb.

Also by George Crabb

Jesus in the Old Testament
Tola'at Shani - The Crimson Worm of Psalm 22

Standalone
Ani Yosef
Road to Emmaus
The Same Today
See Jesus in the Old Testament

Watch for more at www.georgecrabb.com.

Table of Contents

This book is dedicated to my best friend, Lord and King, Jesus
the Messiah.

TOLA'AT SHANI
THE CRIMSON WORM OF PSALM 22
GEORGE CRABB

DEDICATION

To the God of Abraham, Isaac, and Jacob. In Him we can do all things, without Him we can do nothing.
"Come now, and let us reason together, saith the LORD: though your sins be as scarlet (Shani), they shall be as white as snow; though they be red like crimson (Tola'at Shani), they shall be as wool (like a lamb)."
Isaiah 1:18 KJV
(Emphasis added in the parenthesis by the author)
ACKNOWLEDGMENTS
I would like acknowledge my beautiful bride, Christina.

CHAPTER ONE: TOLA'AT SHANI

Tola'at is literally translated "Worm". Shani is translated as, "Scarlet" or "Crimson"...

Therefore, we see it combined as, "Tola'at Shani" to mean, Scarlet Worm, or Crimson Worm.

Today, in Israel, the Temple Institute is making sure that they gather everything needed to build the Jewish Temple. The Institute is committed to the ancient text, to the Law of Moses, by meticulously gathering each item just as the Ancient Israelites did thousands of years ago.

Therefore, their goal is to have all of the elements ready for the quick set up of the Jewish Temple. Just as in king Solomon's day, no hammer or chisel will be heard that day, in the heart of Jerusalem, as they erect the Temple. So, as they constructed and gathered the goods such as; the lamp stand called the Menorah, the table for the showbread, the stones, the gold vessels, the incense, and the priestly garments, something amazing was rediscovered.

This is Israel's mysterious discovery and this is how they found it. They needed to make the scarlet red dye for the veil, and for the High Priest garments just like the times of Moses and King Solomon, when suddenly they discovered the Tola'at Shani.

The Tola'at Shani is translated "Worm" in Hebrew. It is also called the, "Tola'at Shani", translated "Scarlet Worm". This worm was found on trees, then gathered and crushed to make the crimson red dye for the temple fabrics.

The making of the Temple veil and priestly garments requires knowledge of the materials and methods commanded by Torah (the first five books of the Bible written by Moses). So, the knowledge was lost over two-thousand years and had to be researched and relearned.

Just a few years ago, a professor in Israel rediscovered the Tola'at Shani. He said in his own words that it was part of, "the redemptive process of the Jewish people today".

On a hot July day, the Temple Institute organized this historic event: the first Tola'at Shani (crimson worm) harvest in the land of Israel in over 2000 years. The location of the harvest was a hilltop village in Samaria north of Jerusalem. This was the land of the ancient tribe of Ephraim.

The reason for this historical event was the need to gather the crimson-red worms for creating the belt for the priestly garments now being produced by the Temple Institute.

The long-term goal of the event was to educate a new generation in Israel about the elusive Tola'at Shani, how to harvest it, and how to produce the crimson dye prescribed in the Torah.

You see, the Tola'at Shani was used for a number of Temple related purposes, which included the priests' belts, the scarlet wool tied onto the scapegoat on Yom Kippur, and the massive Veil of the Temple.

The lecture about the Tola'at Shani was given by a Professor of a University in Israel. He's a researcher and a world expert in the ancient dye in the Middle East. As he kept the theme focused on the Holy Temple, the professor described his own odyssey with the Tola'at Shani, which he has been intensely researching for ten years.

Studying ancient texts, including the Torah and Talmudic, as well as ancient Greek, Latin and Aramaic works, the professor began to re-identify and re-discover the unique properties and characteristics of the Tola'at Shani. He travelled the world in search of the scarlet worm, and so he discovered the crimson worm being harvested in the mountains of Turkey.

Then something mysterious happened. It was only after his travels abroad that he discovered this Tola'at Shani, were literally a "stone's-throw-away" from his own front door.

The common Israeli oak trees fill much of the hillside land of Israel, and so the tiny crimson Tola'at Shani bodies were attached to them.

So he had a revelation and realized this discovery was just outside his window.

Later the professor explained to the students and some representatives from the Temple Institute, the art of identifying and removing the Tola'at Shani from the bark of the oak trees to which it attaches itself.

The Tola'at Shani attaches itself to the trunk and branches of the oak when it's ready to give birth to its young, this parent Tola'at Shani grows from the size of a pinhead to a maximum of seven millimeters in diameter, which is about the size of a pea.

The many, many tiny crimson eggs develop during the early summer and it is essential to harvest them at this point, before the red eggs hatch and leave the parent, taking with them their crimson-red pigment. The mature parent looks a lot like a miniature Pomegranate fruit when it is ripe.

After the professor finished his lecture, he began to demonstrate by dissolving the Tola'at Shani worms previously harvested and dried, into a glass of boiling water. The results were seen immediately as the glass of clear water turned pink, to dark crimson red like pomegranate juice or red wine.

In fact, the Tola'at Shani is much like a Pomegranate fruit. When the fruit is ripe for harvest, it is full of tiny red seeds (like Tola'at Shani eggs) marked by the same exterior color of the sweet parent fruit. By the way, the Pomegranate was used to make, "Spiced Wine". This is found in King Solomon's, Song of Solomon.

Also, the first Temple in Jerusalem was decorated with Pomegranates. The High Priest also had the Tola'at Shani –dyed yarns made in the shape of the pomegranates sewn onto the hem of his robe.

Interestingly, both the crushed Tola'at Shani, and Pomegranate juice are known for their good medicinal purposes for the heart.

Now, back to our modern day story in Israel. Therefore, the time came to harvest the Tola'at Shani. Although many worms were gathered,

it was still short of the amount needed for the dying of the wool to be embroidered onto the belts of the 120 priestly garments that the Temple Institute is currently producing.

To supplement the supply of Tola'at Shani needed, the Institute sent a group of Israeli's to Ankara, Turkey, to purchase the scarlet worms because they are native to the mountains of Turkey.

Let us imagine this story.

It is around 1,400 years before the birth of Christ. You are a young Hebrew man or women in the camp of Israel with Moses as your leader. You are assigned to collect the Tola'at Shani for the crimson-red dye for the curtains of the tabernacle, and for the priestly garments.

It is hot in the daytime and you are out in the middle of a vast desert called, "The wilderness". Its bone dry for hundreds of miles, so where are you going to find this Tola'at Shani?

The only tree that grows in the middle of the driest deserts are the Acacia trees. They are also the trees that the Lord told Moses to use for the making of the Ark and everything else structural for the tabernacle.

Therefore, you see a few of these Acacia trees outside of the camp and you walk over to one in hope of finding the scarlet worm. The shade of it is relieving as the sun outside of the shade of the camp bakes everything in sight. You are amazed that this tree is able to live and have green leaves in the middle of this parched land.

As you reach up to touch the fine leaves, you feel a sharp prick into the palm of your hand. Blood immediately marks your pierced hand and you notice the tree limbs are covered with thorns - the Acacia tree is also called, "The Thorn Tree".

As you look for the Tola'at Shani on the tree, your skepticism increases as you know they are normally found on the Oak trees. However, you believe that the Lord will provide for the needs of the Tabernacle.

Then you see a tiny Tola'at Shani climb up the trunk of the tree. As it climbs up the trunk to the branches, it clings onto the wood of that

tree. The swollen, brown and red body of the Tola'at Shani is so attached to the tree that you wonder how you will remove it. As you watch the Tola'at Shani, it turns more and more crimson red and it looks like a tiny ripe Pomegranate fruit.

Around three hours after mid-day the Tola'at Shani dies. For some odd reason you feel as if this was the only Tola'at Shani in the world and your sad because it died.

Then you notice tiny scarlet offspring moving about under the body of the parent Tola'at Shani. They eat from the body of their parent, and there are so many of them they appear as innumerable crimson-red fine grain.

You see that the innumerable young Tola'at Shani have gone throughout the entire tree. Their number is great, too many to count. This is good because of the large amount of precious dye needed.

Suddenly, the dead body of the parent Tola'at Shani falls down to the ground like a dead leaf, gliding back and forth in its descent. You followed it with your eyes as it landed right into a small hole in the side of a large rock.

You glance back to the spot where the parent Tola'at Shani gave up its life, in order to give life to its young. The spot is stained scarlet red, as if it was a bloodstain on the trunk of that thorn tree.

You look up past the tree at the rose color hue cast upon the Desert Mountains and realize it is almost the end of the day and you do not want to be late for the Passover meal. Therefore, you run back down to the camp.

As you pass by the outside of the tent city, you sense something in your heart telling you to look back. As you turn your gaze back, you see that "Thorn Tree", that Acacia tree, where the Tola'at Shani is attached. The sun beaming through the cloud cover lights it up. It shines bright like a great fire in the camp; it is so brilliant, and warm. The tree is beautiful, it shimmers like gold, like a golden lamp, yet crowned with thorns.

You pondered these things as you walked toward your father's tent for Passover.

The Passover meal is good and your father gives a great blessing over the meal. With the sun setting, he announces that it is now a new day for us (The Jewish day starts at sunset).

The next day is the Sabbath day. Therefore, the visit to the Acacia tree has to wait for another day. You always enjoy the Sabbath. It is a family time, a time of refreshment and rest. The whole family sleeps in late, tells stories, eats together and laughs together.

After the Passover and Sabbath days, you wake up and realize it is the third day since your visit to the tree and you are so excited to check on the Tola'at Shani.

You wake up early, before the rising of the sun. As you peeled back the opening of the tent, you see that the camp is well lit from the snow-white, frosty looking substance on the ground. Everyone in this tent city calls it, "Manna".

This Manna was an unknown substance but it was delicious and nutritious to eat. Some in the camp call it, "Bread from Heaven". This is because it is from God.

You gather your portion in a basket, and then you run up the snow-white, mana-covered path to see the tree where the Tola'at Shani was found.

"There it is", you thought, as you look at that old rugged tree crowned with many thorns. As the sun rises, you see a bright white spot where the scarlet-red stain had once been. You run your fingertip across the white substance and it felt like soft melted wax.

After some time, a cool breeze picks up, and it lifts that waxy snow-white substance, causing it to fall off the tree to the ground like a snowflake. It looks just like the Manna that "Bread of Heaven", gathered in the camp every morning.

Then you look up, and see a miracle. The numerous offspring of the Tola'at Shani looked fully-grown and ready to be harvested. This is the

perfect amount needed to color the inner curtain, and garments for the priests of the Tabernacle.

You gather a large basket full of these Tola'at Shani (Scarlet worms), and head over to dry them out so that they could be turned into dye. After they were dried, you crush them into a fine powder and as they were being crushed, a sweet aroma arises from this Tola'at Shani.

An old Hebrew woman comes and takes some of the crimson substance to be used for incense. She talks about how the scarlet-red crushed Tola'at Shani is good medicine for the heart. It puts the irregular heartbeat back into the right rhythm.

Later you see a carpenter from the camp carrying a saw. He walks over to the old thorn tree and marks it carefully for the cut. Then one of elders walks over and tells him to make sure to cut the Acacia wood to the proper dimensions, because it was for building the "Ark of the Covenant".

As he carefully falls the old tree, you still see where the once red stain was and it is still as white as snow, but now you see many, many snow-white spots on that tree.

Everybody and everything was coming together for the future Tabernacle. It was a portable place of worship, that dwelling place for the Lord. It was a place where the Lord meets with Moses and his people and shines. His Shakina glory shines out from above a place where the Ark and the Mercy seat were located.

Although this was a fictional story to tell how it played out, it is based on how it was, according to the Scriptures.

A few centuries later, those same preparations would be made for the first Temple in Jerusalem. The people of Israel, under the leadership of King David's son, Solomon, built it.

When Solomon dedicated that Temple to the Lord, the glory of the Lord filled that place, just as the Lord did in the wilderness with Moses, in the camp of Israel.

A few centuries the Babylonians destroyed later that first Temple, just as the Prophet Jeramiah foretold. The Hebrew children were once again taken captive by a Gentile nation.

These Gentiles held the prophet Daniel captive, but he knew that Israel's deliverance would come in the future. He found where the prophet Jeremiah wrote that after seventy years the Jewish people would return to Jerusalem.

Then Daniel had a vision from the Lord that showed him that when the decree comes to restore and rebuild Jerusalem, there would be seven times seven years and seven times sixty-two sevens, which all calculates out to four-hundred and eighty-three years, until the Messiah, the Prince, would come:

"Know therefore and understand, that *from the going forth of the command to restore and build Jerusalem until Messiah the Prince,* there shall be *seven weeks ("Weeks" means "Sevens of years". So seven times seven years equals 49 years) and sixty-two weeks (sixty-two times seven years equals 434 years), The street shall be built again, and the wall, even in troublesome times* (Daniel 9:25).

The decree came from Cyrus the Great, on March 14, 445 BC (Translating the dates from the Jewish calendar). This was recorded in the book of Nehemiah, chapter two.

Then you take that four-hundred and eighty-three years and multiply it by the three-hundred and sixty Jewish prophetic years - which was used in those days – and it brings you to a very interesting date.

It takes you to April 6, 32 AD.

This turns out to be a Sunday, five days before Passover, the same day that a 33-year-old Jewish miracle worker, of the tribe of Judah, entered the East Gate of Jerusalem, riding on a Donkey.

The Jewish people of this time were expecting the Messiah who was to be their savior. Therefore, they yelled out, "Hosanna", which means, "Save now".

His Hebrew name is Yeshua (Joshua).

His name is Jesus in the Greek.

Remember Joshua was the successor of Moses, and he was of the tribe of Ephraim. Which was of the House of Joseph.

Jesus also was from the house of Joseph – His earthly father's name, yet both of Jesus' parents were of the Tribe of Judah by blood.

At this point, you might ask, "I thought the theme of this book is the Tola'at Shani?"

You might ask that, but if you keep reading on, you will see how it all comes together.

So come along and see for yourself.

CHAPTER TWO: psalm 22

"I am a Tola'at Shani"

It was a fresh spring day, and the birds were singing. I sipped my coffee, set the cup down on the table. As I was reading the Psalms from the Dead Sea Scrolls (Oldest known transcripts), I looked at the Hebrew translation of Psalm 22, and how it appeared in the ancient scroll. I was awe-struck at verse six, where David wrote:

"But I am a Tola'at Shani, and no human, scorned by others and despised by the people".

David penned this Psalm one-thousand years before Mary and Joseph saw the sweet shining eyes of their perfect baby boy, Jesus.

As I began to read the whole Psalm from the very beginning, it clearly became alive, right off of the pages. It was as if I was seeing it through the eyes of a Jewish man who was there in Jerusalem, in the first century.

Imagine it. Jerusalem, 0032 CE, we see a devout Jewish man who lived in that ancient city. He was one who studied all of the scriptures, and lived his life following the Law of Moses. We will give him the name, "Benjamin", or just call him "Ben".

Passover day was soon to arrive and Ben wanted to worship the Lord, during this great festival of his people, Israel.

In order to worship properly, Ben purchased a Lamb from the courtyard of the Temple. It was a Lamb without blemish, spotless and white like snow. It was one of the authorized Lambs, raised in the hills of Bethlehem. This is where the Religious leaders had the "approved lambs" raised and then they were brought to Jerusalem.

He paid for and took a cute little Lamb home to his family to live with them at their house in Jerusalem for the next five days.

Ben was a Jewish man who studied the Torah, the words of the Prophets, and the Psalms. He loved all of it but had recently been focusing on the Psalms, written by David.

He read the twenty-second Psalm, and was pondering, and meditating on what David had penned around Millennia ago.

"My God, My God, why have You forsaken Me?
Why are You so far from helping Me,
And from the words of My groaning?
O My God, I cry in the daytime,
But You do not hear;
And in the night season, and am not silent.
But You are holy,
Enthroned in the praises of Israel.
Our fathers trusted in You;
They trusted, and You delivered them.
They cried to You, and were delivered;
They trusted in You, and were not ashamed.
But I am a worm (Tola'at Shani), and no man;
A reproach of men, and despised by the people.
All who see Me ridicule Me,
They shoot out the lip, they shake the head, saying,
"He trusted in the LORD, let Him rescue Him;
Let Him deliver Him, since He delights in Him!"

Ben stopped reading because his heart was troubled. He couldn't understand why David penned these words: "My God, My God, why have You forsaken me". The words sounded over and over in his mind.

"Lord help me to understand this", he prayed out loud in the small upper room of his Jerusalem home.

"But I am a worm (Tola'at Shani), and no man", he said over and over. Then he whispered, "What did David mean, 'I am a Tola'at Shani and no man', and what does it mean Lord?"

After he pondered these things for some time, he rolled up the scroll and looked out his window at the golden, rocky hillside spotted with olive trees and oak trees. The spring air was fragrant and refreshing.

Then Ben turned around and saw his little lamb resting near the corner stone of his house. The lamb was silent, just looking at Ben with innocent brown eyes. Then Ben said, "You poor little guy, I am sad that you have to be sacrificed for our sins in a few days, but it must be so."

Thursday night came quickly and Ben was excited to go to the Temple to worship God on Passover the next day. He knew that the sacrifice of the Lamb would atone for his sins and allow him to worship in the Temple of God.

That night he woke suddenly to the sound of many men laughing and cursing loudly in the street below, just outside his upper-room window. He saw a man bound by the neck with heavy chains and a sackcloth over his head. He was being punched in the head, and spat at by the guards as they moved him down the narrow street.

The man was silent, and seemed to be in control and focused on going along with these brutal men. Ben looked over to the other side of the room and saw his lamb again, looking at him with those same eyes, just staying silent and peaceful.

The noise of the large group of temple guards faded away as they went down the narrow cobble stone road, down toward the southwestern section of the city.

The morning sun was warm, golden and bright. Ben was a late riser and after spending a good amount of time in his morning prayers, he tied a rope around his lamb to walk it up to the Temple.

Ben saw a steady stream of blood mixed with water flowing out of the temple courtyard toward the side of the East Gate.

There at the entrance to the of the magnificent Temple, was a priest who started inspecting, examining, and criticizing the lamb who was with him. Not once did the priest scrutinize or examine Ben, he only criticized the lamb and he found no fault or blemish, so Ben entered in.

At that moment, he heard a large crowd up near the northwest corner of the outer courtyard. He saw the Roman Leader named, Pontius Pilate shouting, "I find no fault in him".

Then Ben walked closer and saw a man swollen from beatings. He was scourged and bruised so much that his skin was scarlet. Someone said it was the Galilean, that Jewish teacher named Jesus. He was bound in chains and beaten badly, but was as silent as Ben's lamb.

Then the crowd erupted in loud shouting and Ben could hear many of them say, "May his blood be upon us and our children". Others shouted, "Crucify him".

This was too much drama for Ben so he walked away to the uncrowded entrance of the Temple. He met one of the working priests there who immediately focused all of his attention on the lamb walking next to Ben.

Then the priest took the Lamb from Ben. This hurt because the lamb had become a part of Ben's life. The lamb played with his children, and cuddled with him and his wife. They fed it, hugged it and felt like it was part of their family over the last five days.

So Ben watched as his lamb, the one that knew him and he knew, was being sacrificed. It was sacrificed for his sins and the sins of his family. It was not an easy thing to see, but it gave him assurance that the blood of that lamb covered those sins.

Now Ben was free to worship the God of Abraham, Isaac, and Jacob. His sins were atoned for and he was free. He raised his hands up into the air, looking up at the blue sky with joy in his heart.

Ben was in deep worship singing the Psalms, having great fellowship with his brethren, and spending good time in prayer.

As he was praying, something happened. The afternoon sky suddenly turned dark, very dark. People around him started to fear and tremble, and then one of them yelled out, "God is angry because we have rejected Jesus of Nazareth".

After it had turned strangely dark, Ben walked out of the western exit of the temple area. He looked up on the hillside and saw three crosses. As he walked up the hill called, Golgotha" he felt that something so immense and intense was happening that it was as all of nature was holding its breath.

He was drawn to the crucifixion site and walked up the narrow stone road to the top of hill. Ben noticed a crimson stained flow of water trickling its way down the stone road from the crucifixion site. He remembered the similar flow from out or the temple earlier.

As soon as he was close, about a stone's throw away, he looked up at the center cross. There he was, Jesus of Nazareth, his body was swollen and crimson red, with a sign above his head written in Hebrew, Aramaic, and Greek stating, and "This is Jesus of Nazareth, the King of the Jews".

Ben noticed acacia thorns weaved together and pushed down onto Jesus' head as if it were a crown. It was as if His cross was a "Thorn Tree", as the Acacia tree is called. Ben's heart hurt for this Jesus, and his eyes began to well up with sorrow.

Then Jesus' head moved up and he shouted out, *"My God, My God, why have you forsaken me".*

Immediately Ben knew that Jesus was saying the beginning words to Psalm twenty-two.

Ben knew that Psalm well. He never really understood it but now he was watching the Psalm play out in real time before his eyes.

Ben began to say the rest of the Psalm to finish what Jesus started, *"Why are You so far from helping Me, and from the words of My groaning?"* As Ben said that, Jesus groaned in deep pain.

Then Ben continued to whisper the Psalm, *"O My God, I cry in the daytime, but You do not hear; And in the night season, and am not silent."* Ben looked around and realized it was as dark as night, and he realized the fulfillment of the prophetic Psalm of David.

Ben continued, *"But You are holy, enthroned in the praises of Israel. Our fathers trusted in You; They trusted, and You delivered them. They cried to You, and were delivered; They trusted in You, and were not ashamed."*

Ben gasped as he began to say the next verse: *"But I am a worm (Tola'at Shani), and no man".*

Ben fell to his knees in amazement. He looked up to Jesus and saw the crimson bloodstain on Jesus' body and on the wood of the cross.

Ben knew the meaning of the Tola'at Shani in David's prophetic writing at this very moment.

You see, Ben was Jerusalem's main yarn and dye dealer. He was known as the renowned expert in dyes and the Religious leaders of the Temple depended on him to get the Tola'at Shani, the red dye for the Veil of the Temple and the Priestly garments.

Ben knew that the Tola'at Shani would attach itself to a tree when it was ready to die. He knew it would do this to give life to its young. He knew that the Tola'at Shani would turn blood red, and stain the surrounding wood of the tree red.

Then Ben started remembering other areas in the scriptures where this word Tola'at Shani was. He stood to his feet and quoted from Judges, then Isaiah:

"There arose to save Israel Tola'at Shani..." (Judges 10)

"Come now, and let us reason together, saith the LORD: though your sins be as scarlet (Shani), they shall be as white as snow; though they be red like crimson (Tola'at Shani), they shall be as wool." (Isaiah 1:18)

Then he looked around and noticed many of the Religious leaders shaking their heads, despising and ridiculing Jesus. Then the Psalm was made real again and Ben quoted it, *"A reproach of men, and despised by the people. All who see Me ridicule Me; They shoot out the lip, they shake the head, saying, 'He trusted in the LORD, let Him rescue Him; Let Him deliver Him, since He delights in Him!'"*

At that very moment one of the religious leaders said, *"He trusted in God; let him deliver him now, if he will have him: for he said, I am the Son of God."*

Ben began to weep. He knew at this moment that this man named Yeshua, this man, Jesus of Nazareth was in fact the Son of God.

He could barely take it all in, but Ben was compelled in his heart and soul to cling to this truth and so he remembered the rest of the Psalm: *"But You* are *He who took Me out of the womb; You made Me trust* while *on My mother's breasts"*. As Ben whispered this scripture, Jesus saw his mother standing next to John. John was the closest disciple to Jesus, and as Jesus hung on the cross, He said to His mother, *"Woman, behold your son!"*

Ben continued the Psalm, *"I was cast upon You from birth. From My mother's womb You My God. Be not far from Me, For trouble* is *near; For there is none to help. Many bulls have surrounded Me; Strong bulls of Bashan have encircled Me. They gape at Me with their mouths, Like a raging and roaring lion."* At that moment, Ben sensed something greater than the physical crucifixion was happening. There was a darkness greater than the physical darkness that surrounded the scene; this was more as Hell was taking over the earth.

Ben looked at Jesus and noticed the blood pouring out like water from his wounds. Then he saw that his shoulders were out of joint. This recalled the Psalm once again, *"I am poured out like water, and all My bones are out of joint; My heart is like wax; It has melted within Me."*

Then Jesus cried out, *"I thirst"*. At that moment Ben recalled the Psalm, *"My strength is dried up like a potsherd, And My tongue clings to My jaws; You have brought Me to the dust of death."*

Ben watched and whispered the Psalm as it played out before his eyes, *"For dogs have surrounded Me; The congregation of the wicked has enclosed Me. They pierced My hands and My feet; I can count all My bones. They look* and *stare at Me."*

Ben looked over to where the Roman soldiers were and he saw them casting lots for Jesus' clothing. It was as if the Psalm was passed out to everyone on the scene as a script and they played their part perfectly.

Therefore, Ben whispered it while watching the soldiers, *"They divide My garments among them, and for My clothing they cast lots."*

Then Jesus said, *"It is finished (Paid in full)"*, and his head bowed down and he died.

Ben knew that Jesus had just quoted the last word in Psalm 22, "Asah" in Hebrew; or "Tetelestai" in the Greek both meaning, "Finished" and "Paid in full".

Ben's heart was broken.

Suddenly a deep roar came from deep within the earth; everything began to shake violently because this was a powerful earthquake. It was so powerful that entire boulders split in two.

Then a priest from the Temple came over and yelled out, "The veil that separates the Holiest place was torn from top to bottom."

Then the soldiers were ordered to break the legs of all three of them being crucified. They did so to cause them to die right away because they would not be able to push up with their legs to breathe. However, when they came to Jesus they noticed he was already dead, so they did not break his legs.

Then Ben recalled a different Psalm, *"He guards all his bones; Not one of them is broken."*

Ben looked at Jesus' crimson-stained, bruised body and saw the many stripes on Him. Then as they lowered Him down from the cross, he recalled the scripture from Isaiah the prophet, *"But He* was *wounded for our transgressions, He was bruised for our iniquities; The chastisement for our peace* was *upon Him, and by His stripes we are healed."*

Ben sat down on the smooth stone pavement and understood how magnanimous this moment was. He remembered the verse in the Psalm, *"But I am a Tola'at Shani, and no man, a reproach of men, and despised of the people.*

"But I am a Tola'at Shani", he thought. A Tola'at Shani, that tiny creature that dies, stuck to the tree. It marks the wood blood red, then its offspring eat of its flesh. They go out into the world marked with that same crimson color.

Then he remembered that after three days, that blood-red stain on the tree turns as white as snow and glides to the ground like a snow flake, and so he remembered Isaiah, *"Come now, and let us reason together, says the LORD: though your sins be as scarlet (Shani), they shall be as white as snow; though they be red like crimson (Tola'at Shani), they shall be as wool (like a lamb)."*

Ben reflected on how nature itself proclaimed the glory of the Lord, and so Ben uttered, *"Tola'at Shani the Great".*

Let us pause and look at this.

Men are never good let alone great, but Jesus is good and great.

Alexander the Great?

No.

Herod the Great?

No.

Napoleon the Great?

Really?

No way!

Jesus is Great. He is the Savior and He is God the Son. Therefore, it is really, "Jesus the Great".

King David wrote this one-thousand years before it was fulfilled and played out in Jesus' time. Many witnessed the scene but few understood that it was being fulfilled in order and according to the ancient scriptures.

We can see another scripture with "Tola'at Shani" in it: 1st Chronicles, chapter seven, *"The sons of Tola'at Shani were mighty men of valor in their generations; their number in the days of David was twenty-two thousand six hundred".*

In that scripture we saw the name David (The Psalmist), then we saw twenty-two (Psalm 22), we saw a thousand (Psalm 22 was written 1000 years Before Christ), then we saw six (Verse 6). We also saw the words, "The sons of Tola'at Shani".

That scripture was not numbered by mistake, nor was it written by chance. I believe God inspired it, to show a pattern to His people.

The sons of Tola'at Shani, mighty men of valor, in the days of David the Psalmist, numbered twenty-two thousand six hundred. Wow!

It is as if the Holy Spirit took a highlighter pen to mark on this scripture and to magnify its significance, "Look here in the Chronicles, then look at the Psalm, and look at history and see it for yourself".

CHAPTER THREE: grain

Jesus said, *"The hour has come that the Son of Man should be glorified. Most assuredly, I say to you, unless a grain of wheat falls into the ground and dies, it remains alone; but if it dies, it produces much grain. He who loves his life will lose it, and he who hates his life in this world will keep it for eternal life. If anyone serves Me, let him follow Me; and where I am, there My servant will be also. If anyone serves Me, him My Father will honor.*

"Now My soul is troubled, and what shall I say? 'Father, save Me from this hour'? But for this purpose I came to this hour. Father, glorify Your name."

Then a voice came from heaven, saying, "I have both glorified it and will glorify it again." (John 12)

Look at the words of Jesus, *"Most assuredly, I say to you, unless a grain of wheat falls into the ground and dies, it remains alone; but if it dies, it produces much grain."* He also said, *"But for this purpose, I came..."*. He said all of this, referring to his death on the cross.

This proves to the world that it was not the Jewish people, the Romans, the World, the nails, Satan or his minions who put Jesus on the cross.

No.

It was Jesus Himself and His Father, who put Him on that cross.

Why?

Because He loves you, and me. It was God's great love for us, to pay for our sins in full, once and for all. It was "Asah" (paid in full). It was at that moment when the prophetic Psalm was fulfilled and the greatest deed of love was birthed.

Just as the Tola'at Shani clung to the tree to give life to its young, so too Jesus clung Himself to that cross to give life to you and me. Now we can be born again as a new creature, birth marked by his Scarlet blood, as one of His, a son of Tola'at Shani, so to speak. Then we become His grain.

He is Christ, the Messiah.

We are "Little Christs", as Christians. We are, "The body of Christ".

He is Tola'at Shani the Great.

We are "Little Tola'at Shani's".

We are sons and daughters of Tola'at Shani.

In Europe during the middle ages (5th to 15th centuries) the red dye for the exquisite silks came from the rich crimson and carmine red colors of the Tola'at Shani. They live on the sap of certain trees, especially the Kermes Oak tree near the Mediterranean region, in countries like Turkey and Israel.

The English names for red colors such as, "Crimson" and "Carmine" are derived from the word Kermes. The Tola'at Shani is also known as the "Kermes Worm".

During the middle ages the rich crimson and scarlet colored silks were dyed by using the Kermes dye. The silk weaving centers of Italy and Sicily started using the Kermes dye, which exceeded the legendary Tyrian purple of that time in both status and desirability.

This newfound dyestuff was called, "Grain" in all Western European languages, because the tiny eggs resembled fine grains of wheat like sand. So the textiles dyed with Kermes were described as, "Dyed in the grain".

What a great picture, right?

Jesus said, "Most assuredly, I say to you, unless a grain of wheat falls into the ground and dies, it remains alone; but if it dies, it produces much grain."

We, who abide in Jesus, are under His care, His shelter, and are His grain, His dyestuff.

We are also His harvest.

One summer I was driving down a beautiful country road near my house. It was a warm, late summer afternoon, and I noticed the wheat field shimmering in the afternoon wind. It was fully-grown and ready for harvest, so the heads of grain were bowed down and the entire grain field was shining like gold as it glimmered in the sun's light. What a beautiful picture of God's people.

The Kermes (Tola'at Shani) dyestuff was called "Grain" in all of Europe, because it resembled fine grain or sand.

In that same way the "Born-again" followers of Jesus, are His grain and so the Church is His grain field.

Jesus said, "I am the bread of life".

The church is called, "The body of Christ". We are in essence His, "Organic, Whole Grain".

Believers in Jesus are called His true church. We are not a denomination, organization or a building. His Church are simply His followers who are in Him, representing His body marked by His blood.

As I was typing this page in my home, it was an ice-cold, stormy, windy day here in the Pacific Northwest. My wife suddenly asked me to open the garage. She never asks me to do this so I asked her "why"? She did not really know why, but I opened our garage door anyway.

Five minutes later, while typing this manuscript I heard our kitchen door open from the stormy outside and suddenly an old man's voice saying, "Will you help me, I am lost".

I ran quickly into the kitchen where my son and wife were having lunch and saw an old man, who was shivering, cold, and scared.

I walked him home, and as we walked he said that he would pay me back for helping him. I said, "No need my friend it's grace. You owe me nothing. I am a follower of Jesus, and He gives me grace, He gives me life in Him forever which I don't deserve nor could I ever repay".

The old man looked at me as we neared his house, smiled, and said, "I follow Jesus as well. He comes to my bedside and talks to me sometimes." This was a miracle, because of how it all fit together. After all, I was writing about how the true followers of Jesus love to help the helpless.

Today we see the Jewish nation of Israel being the ridicule of most of the world. They are being bullied by the surrounding countries and the United Nations.

Christians, who are His "Grain", His "Dye stuff", are marked by his blood and so we need to remember Jesus' own country, Israel, and His kindred the Jews. We must remember the cross had a sign posted above His head, "Jesus of Nazareth King of the Jews".

We may presently be in the "Church Age", or the "Time of the Gentiles", but God hasn't forgotten His beloved people, Israel.

Jesus is called our Great High Priest. Look at this in the book of Hebrews, "Seeing then that we have a great High Priest who has passed through the heavens, Jesus the Son of God, let us hold fast *our* confession."

The High Priest would ensure the Golden Lamp stand with the seven lamps called the Menorah, was kept lit. He would feed olive oil into the Menorah which kept the wicks burning bright. As he did this, we can imagine the inside of that Holy Place was bright because the light reflected off the gold furnishings.

As the High Priest kept the seven lamp stands burning bright with the oil, the breastplate on his chest would light up. The breastplate was made of pure gold and had twelve precious stones embedded into it. These twelve jewels were representative of the twelve tribes of Israel.

This breastplate was strategically placed over the heart of the High Priest.

Therefore, Jesus, our Great High Priest keeps His seven churches (Revelation 2-3), alive and shining bright by the anointing oil and fire of the Holy Spirit. As He keeps our hearts burning bright, the twelve tribes of Israel are on Jesus' heart the whole time.

Israel is on His heart right now.

Israel never left His heart.

When His Church shines brighter by the abundant oil, the twelve precious stones shine brighter over his heart. The churches who love and help Israel burn with God's love in their hearts and shine brightly into the world.

This takes us to the true and real present day story in chapter one of this book.

Remember how the professor, the students, and the Temple Institute Representatives were rediscovering the Tola'at Shani?

This Rabbi and professor in Israel expressed the rediscovery of the Tola'at Shani as part of the redemptive process of the Jewish people today.

Then the time came to harvest the Tola'at Shani in the land of Israel. Although many scarlet worms were gathered, it was still short of the amount needed for the coloring of the wool to be embroidered onto the belts of the 120 priestly garments that the Temple Institute is currently producing.

To supplement the supply of Tola'at Shani needed, the Temple Institute had sent a group of Israeli's to Ankara, Turkey, to purchase the Tola'at Shani that are native to the mountains of Turkey.

Now, what is interesting is the amount needed had to be supplemented by purchasing the Tola'at Shani from the mountains of Turkey. These mountains were the very place where the early Church began. This area in the Roman Empire was called, "Asia Minor". To be even more specific, the city of Ankara was the very place of the Galatians. This is one of the greatest books in the New Testament written by the great Jewish man of Jesus named Paul.

The book of Galatians is perhaps the best book for the Jewish man or women to understand how Jesus fulfilled the Law.

So we might find that very interesting, that the Israelites of today, went to that very place to purchase the "Dyestuff", the "Grain", and the "Tola'at Shani" to help build fabric for the new Temple in Jerusalem.

You see, the Church is the Gentile Bride of Christ. Jesus is the Great High Priest. Remember, the seven golden lamps were kept lit and maintained by the High Priest. He was near and next to the Menorah. This is a great illustration of the Bride of Christ.

Today, we are in the Church Age, the "Time of the Gentiles". Jesus talked about this to his disciples, *"And Jerusalem will be trampled by the Gentiles until the times of the Gentiles are fulfilled." (Luke 21:24)*

Paul expounded further on this in Romans chapter 11:

"For I do not desire, brethren, that you should be ignorant of this mystery, lest you should be wise in your own opinion, that blindness in part has happened to Israel until the fullness of the Gentiles has come in. And so all Israel will be saved as it is written..."

The "Time of the Gentiles" is the "Church Age".

Go to Rome today, and you will see an Ancient Archway that was dedicated to Titus. He was the Roman General who destroyed Jerusalem in 70 AD. Carved on the archway is a scene of the Roman soldiers carrying the Menorah and the Table for the Showbread from the Temple in Jerusalem.

In the carved image, we see what God had already allowed to happen. You see, the Romans thought they had conquered Jerusalem and that the "Seven Golden Lampstands" were at that moment brought to Rome. However, the truth is, God had already moved the "Seven Lamps" into the Roman province of Asia Minor (Modern day Turkey).

The "Church of Jerusalem" was no longer in Jerusalem after 70 AD.

You see, Paul had already spread the good news and planted the seven churches that Jesus addressed in Revelation chapters 2-3. Revelation also describes the seven golden lampstands as the seven churches.

Pictures and patterns of Jesus are found in all of the ancient scriptures. From Moses, the Prophets, the Psalms we find Him.

A "Scarlet Thread" weaves through the entire Bible. This thread is dyed by the crushing of the Tola'at Shani, just like Isaiah 53 foretold the details of the Messiah. Just look at how it was written in the "Dead Sea Scrolls" (Written over 100 years Before Christ):

"But He was wounded for our transgressions, He was crushed for our iniquities..."

He was crushed for our sins and the Tola'at Shani was crushed to produce the "Scarlet Thread". The scarlet-dyed thread was tied to the "Scapegoat", and then it was sent eastward out so far that it would never be seen again. The blood of Jesus casts our sins cast away as, "Far as the east is from the west", the Bible says.

We also see in Joshua, the story of Rehab. She was a Gentile woman who was saved by hanging the "Scarlet Cord" out of her window. This cord was made of the, Tola'at Shani-dyed thread. She then married into the Jewish family, and became the great grandmother of King David, who was of the direct lineage of Jesus' mother Mary.

Let us just look at Joseph as another story showing the "Scarlet Thread" of Jesus:

Joseph had a miraculous birth by the father's favored wife. Joseph was the father's favored son.

He was despised and rejected by his own brothers.

He told his own, Israel's sons, about his dreams. In his dreams, they were bowing down to him. Therefore, they hated him even more, because of his dreams.

The father sent him out of Hebron (means fellowship) to check on and report to him about his brothers.

They conspired to kill him. They sold him for pieces of silver. They took his tunic from him and it was bloodied. They handed him over to the Gentiles.

He was falsely accused. The Gentile leader had him condemned.

Two were condemned with him. He told them their fate, and one died a cursed death, but the other lived and was restored to the King.

He was raised up and out of that place called the pit. He then stood before the throne, in clean clothing and only he was found worthy to reveal God's plan.

The king gave him glory and honor. Then the king gave him a Gentile Bride.

The king gave him all authority under his throne. All the people had to bow down to him except he who sat on the throne.

He also gave him a new name, which means, "Savior of the World".

He was in charge of gathering grain to save the world. He gathered so much grain; it was innumerable like the sands of the sea.

His Gentile Bride was safe with him before that 7 year worldwide famine began. When that troubled time came, he saved many, as the great famine was over all the face of the earth. People cried out for help to the king on the throne (Pharaoh), but he told them to go to his right hand man Joseph, who was in charge of the grain houses.

During this time, Jacob's trouble came as the whole family was going to die from the famine. Therefore, Israel (Jacob) sent his sons, who were the brothers of the "Savior of the World" who was in charge of the grain, whom they had left for dead many years ago. However, this time, instead of rejecting him, they came bowed down to the ground, in fulfillment of his dreams.

The man in charge was still their brother, and his heart broke the moment he saw his brothers.

They came to buy grain to save their family of Israel. They did not know, or recognize him at first. They thought he was dead long, long ago.

He graciously gave them grain for food to save them. Then they came again and he revealed who he was to them.

He said, "Ani Yosef" – "I am Joseph".

Someday Jesus will say, "Ani Yeshua" – "I am Jesus".

They were afraid, dismayed and shocked. He then asked his brothers to come closer. He spoke to them again, "Ani Yosef, don't be afraid".

They did not know it, but he had already forgiven them. He hugged each one them and wept over them. He told them, "God meant for all of it to happen the way it did to save their lives". He said to them that it was not they who sent him to Egypt, but God.

He then sent them back with grain, and supplies. He gave all of Israel's family new clothing and chariots to bring them to him. He had them brought back to him to live richly, and abundantly. In the best of the land, they all lived together for a long time.

He saved his whole family from the great famine. This famine, this time of great trouble was over the face of the entire earth. Imagine it. It was for seven long years.

Therefore, he took care of the whole family of Israel, and saved them. It was a great deliverance from the burning famine. He then blessed them with homes in the best of the land.

He had his wife and two sons united and grafted into the family of Israel.

They lived together as one family, all because of God's great plan through his man, Joseph.

Can you see the pattern?

Joseph was a great picture of the real savior, the Lord Jesus Christ.

The Bible is the best commentary for the Bible. Man has his theories and interpretations, but the Bible speaks loud and clear through the ancient stories like Joseph's.

In the book of Joshua, we see more illustrations of Christ. We see it illustrated when Rahab the Harlot, tied the "Scarlet Cord" from out of her home.

Joshua is the Hebrew name for Jesus. Therefore, the army of Joshua (Jesus) was coming to destroy, but by believing and identifying herself with the "Scarlet Cord", Rahab was saved from the coming wrath. No doubt, this Scarlet Cord was made by the dye of the Tola'at Shani.

Rahab the Gentile, became a bride to a Jewish man and married into the family of Israel. She became "Grafted-in", so to speak, into God's family. Her descendants included, Boaz, Jessie, King David, and down the line to Mary and Joseph. Then we see born in Bethlehem, by the Virgin Mary, Jesus (Joshua).

Speaking of the scarlet cord, remember our fictional character in chapter two named Ben?

Let us imagine again, as Ben watched Jesus crucified, he saw the cord, the rope used for hoisting up the cross was still hanging there from Jesus' cross. The rope was now colored Scarlet from Jesus' precious blood. While Ben saw this, he thought of Rehab's story as the Scarlet Cord waved back and forth in the wind from the cross.

We have all been taught the bad in Church History. Our professors, teachers, politicians, and authors have showed us all of the evil acts. However, what about the good, fruitful works of His people?

Church history started with the Jewish Church of Jerusalem, then to the early first century Gentile early churches of Rome's, Asia Minor (modern day Turkey). After that, we see that the Church expanded throughout the entire world.

By the way, the countries today that are majority Christian have a common cultural impact in one very important area. They treat women as human beings and not as property. It was Jesus who changed how women were looked at forever.

Just look at how women are treated in Muslim countries compared to the countries with Christian roots.

In Israel, Europe, North and South America, women can vote, dress how they want, speak out publically, and run for high office in their government.

The history of the church started after the resurrection of Jesus all the way to today. It's been almost 2000 years since that amazing day of His resurrection.

We see it recorded in the book of Luke, chapter 24, that the resurrected Jesus walked for seven miles on the road to Emmaus with two of His followers. He taught them where he was shown in all of the scriptures. We can imagine Jesus taught them Joseph's story, Isaiah 53, and Psalm 22. For more insight take a look at my book "Road to Emmaus".

After the ascension of Jesus to Heaven, it was fifty days later that the Holy Spirit descended upon the apostles, just as Jesus had promised.

This transformed them from men cowering with fear, hiding themselves behind locked doors, into bold preachers of the good news of Jesus.

The early church of Jerusalem was powerful. Peter, James, John, and the other disciples of Jesus had fire in their hearts to share the good news. It was great news that Jesus Christ made a way for us sinners to go to heaven.

Later, Jesus used the apostle Paul, of the tribe of Benjamin greatly. This last apostle made the complete number of twelve, and he was a Benjamite.

Interesting, isn't it?

Joseph was a living illustration of Jesus and he loved his youngest brother Benjamin and gave him five times the blessing. Paul penned two thirds of the New Testament, and so it seems that this Benjamite received a greater blessing as well.

So the message of the cross, the death and resurrection of the Son of God, was paramount. They preached Jesus to the public and many were saved. They traveled throughout the Roman Empire, which in turn spread it to the whole world.

Christianity survived and blossomed as a sweet fruit of new life despite the aroused wrath of the Roman Empire. The attacks became severe as James; who was John's brother, was the first apostle to be killed for preaching Jesus.

Later, Paul spread the good news to many parts of the Roman Empire and planted many churches. He wrote 66 percent of the New Testament including the powerful book of Romans.

In Romans chapter 11, it is clear that God keeps his promises to the Jewish people. It was made clear that He would restore them and save a remnant. Interestingly Jesus fed the 5,000 Jewish people in the Jewish area around the Sea of Galilee and there were 12 remaining baskets of bread. Remember there were 12 tribes of Israel. This speaks of a remnant, not consumed but saved by God.

When Jesus fed the 7,000 Gentile people in the Greek area, on the east side of the Sea of Galilee, there were seven baskets of bread remaining. Remember there are seven churches listed in the book of Revelation.

Today, we see Israel restored to their homeland and in control of Jerusalem. Amazing, isn't it? This miracle has actually happened in our modern time.

Let us take a quick journey, an overview of early church history.

AD 65 – 68. During the rule and persecution of Nero, the big fisherman Peter was martyred. According to tradition, Peter didn't believe he was worthy to die like his Savior, so he asked to be crucified upside down.

Around this same time Roman, authorities also arrested Paul. Since it was illegal to crucify a Roman citizen, this is likely why Paul died by the sword.

AD 67. The Romans attacked the region of Galilee. General Vespasian and his son Titus led the attack. They both ended up becoming Emperors.

AD 70. Jerusalem falls and the Romans destroyed the Temple. Not one stone of the Temple remained on another just as Jesus had foretold. There is physical evidence of this in Jerusalem today, as well as in the writings of Josephus.

Eventually all of the apostles of Jesus were killed except for one. His name was John. He was probably the closest follower of Jesus. He was the only disciple who was there on the hill, at the foot of the cross as Jesus died.

History records that in AD 95; John was arrested during the reign of Emperor Domitian and sentenced to be submerged in boiling oil. Miraculously, the blistering hot oil did not hurt him because when he emerged he was completely unharmed. Some say he preached about Jesus the entire time and many gave their lives to Jesus.

This frightened the superstitious Romans and they did not know what to do, so they banished that old man named John, to the island of Patmos. However, John was not left alone because during his harsh imprisonment, Jesus appeared to him in a vision and revealed to him future events.

After his release from Patmos, John served Jesus as the last living apostle, and so he lived in the city of Ephesus. It was there, that he wrote about his life with Jesus. By the Holy Spirit, he wrote his gospel account, three letters, and the prophetic last book of the Bible, the final events of world history revealed to him at Patmos, called the book of Revelation.

It is recorded in history that near the end of John's life, people would travel from far to see and listen to this last living disciple of Jesus. Many in the crowd at the church in Ephesus to hear John preach. As they carried the old man in and sat him down, John would pray a blessing over the crowd. The crowd waited in great anticipation for the sermon, to hear this great man expound through the scriptures.

Near the end of his life, he started his sermons and ended them with these five words, "Little children love one another".

Many were disappointed at him because of this. It got tedious, people were expecting a long sermon and so they complained. Tradition says one man came to him and said, "Brother John, might you bring us something deeper?"

John replied, "Jesus gave us that command, and it doesn't get any deeper."

Shortly after that, John died of a natural death at a ripe old age, possibly one hundred years old.

AD 135, the Emperor Hadrian blotted out the name "Provincia Judea" and renamed it "Provincia Syria Palaestina (Palestine)". So this evil Emperor hated the Jewish people so deeply that he renamed the land,

"Palestine" to try to wipe Israel and Judea off the map (much like Israel's enemies proclaim today).

Following Hadrian's death in 138 AD, the Romans banned Jews from Jerusalem. The historian Josephus wrote, "The majority of the Jewish population of Judea was either killed, exiled, or sold."

Therefore, the Jewish people were dispersed throughout the world.

Later the land of "Judah", or "Israel", was renamed "Southern Syria" by the Arabs, then renamed "Palestine".

AD 138 - 300. Great persecution by the Roman Emperors continued, but the Church or "Grain" multiplied and grew. The Church is called "The Body of Christ", and Jesus is the Bread of Life.

AD 300, to today.

Sure, church history is marred. However, no one seems to focus on the good works of the Christians.

Hospitals started because of true Christians.

The Christians started universities.

Orphanages started by the Christians.

A Christian man named William Wilberforce spearheaded abolishing slavery in Britain. He was encouraged by John Newton, who was a slave trader but became a Christian. Newton wrote the powerful hymn called, "Amazing Grace".

Later, a Christian man named Abraham Lincoln freed the slaves in America.

It was mostly the Christians who hid the Jewish people of Europe from the evil Nazis. My great uncle was one of those who helped the Jewish people. When I was a little boy, he joyfully showed me the tattooed number on the inside of his arm, signifying his time inside a concentration camp. He had no toes because the Nazis made him walk barefoot in the frigid snow.

Professors have taught that the Nazis and the Crusaders were Christians. They may have called themselves Christians, but their evil works give them away.

Jesus said, *"A good tree cannot bear bad fruit, nor can a bad tree bear good fruit. Every tree that does not bear good fruit is cut down and thrown into the fire. Therefore by their fruits you will know them.*

Not everyone who says to Me, 'Lord, Lord,' shall enter the kingdom of heaven, but he who does the will of My Father in heaven. Many will say to Me in that day, 'Lord, Lord, have we not prophesied in Your name, cast out demons in Your name, and done many wonders in Your name?' And then I will declare to them, 'I never knew you; depart from Me, you who practice lawlessness!' (Matthew 7)

When those who murdered people in the Inquisition and in Nazi concentration camps say they did it in His name, Jesus will say, "I never knew you".

Jesus knows His people and His people know Him. His people are still sinners, and we will fall from time to time. However, we will get back up and produce good fruit.

That fruit is love.

The fruit of the Spirit is love.

CHAPTER 4: AROSE TO SAVE israel

This final chapter will give you great hope.

*After Abimelech there arose to save Israel **Tola'at Shani** the son of Puah, the son of Dodo...* (Judges 10)

The name, "*Abimelech*" means, "My father is king".

We know **Tola'at Shani** means "Scarlet Worm".

The name, "*Puah*" means "Splendid".

The name, "*Dodo*" means "His beloved".

Therefore, we can paraphrase this scripture by plugging in the meanings:

"After my Father is King there arose to save Israel the Scarlet Worm the Son of Splendid, the Son of His beloved..."

Jesus had a sign above his head on the cross stating, "Jesus of Nazareth, King of the Jews". This sign was not ripped in two like the Temple Veil, when it was torn from top to bottom, the moment Jesus died.

Today, as I am writing this down, "Jesus the Son of Splendid", is and always will be "The King of the Jews" and the "Savior of Israel".

Now let us take a look at something that is typically overlooked by most Christians. It's called the Jubilee.

Here is how it started. Starting way back with Moses, God showed him how to establish the Jubilee.

This is how it works.

After working the land for six years, the land and the workers were to rest on the seventh year. Therefore, they would store up double the harvest on the sixth year and just take a yearlong vacation on the seventh.

Wouldn't you love that?

A whole year off!

Yes. That is exactly what God intended for us. It was just like the Sabbath day, that seventh day, a day of rest, but this was a whole year of rest. Remember Jesus said, "the Sabbath was for man, not man for the Sabbath." So too, the seventh year was the same thing.

By the way, farmers use this to this day. They work the land and grow crops for six straight years, then on the seventh, they rest the land. This works best for the soil of the land.

So, the great Jubilee described in Leviticus takes it deeper, much deeper. A series of seven Jubilee years; 7x7 equals 49 years. Right after that 49th year (which was the seventh Jubilee), we have the 50th year, which is where we have this great Jubilee year. Therefore, you would actually get two years off every 50 years.

However, it gets even better. Not only do you get a two-year vacation, on top of that, all debts are wiped away, just gone, forgotten. However, wait, there's more. You also were set free, to return back to your homeland, to be reunited with your family and friends. It was all about a homecoming, freedom, and restoration.

Leviticus 25:9-10

"Then you shall cause the trumpet of the Jubilee to sound on the tenth day of the seventh month; on the Day of Atonement you shall make the trumpet to sound throughout all your land.

And you shall consecrate the fiftieth year, and proclaim liberty throughout all the land to all its inhabitants. It shall be a Jubilee for you; and each of you shall return to his possession, and each of you shall return to his family."

The trumpet sounds, and the great family reunion begins.

Leviticus 27:21

"but the field, when it is released in the Jubilee, shall be holy to the LORD, as a devoted field; it shall be the possession of the priest."

Jesus is our Great High Priest.

We have been talking about the "Grain Stuff", the great harvest of God, the sound of the Trumpet. It all sounds like the great gathering of God's people, much like Joseph gathering the grain, and the scene John saw in Revelation. Remember there were so many, they were like the sands of the sea, without number.

Isaiah 48 shows us a picture of the, "Grain":

"Thus says the LORD, your redeemer, the Holy One of Israel...Your descendants also would have been like the sand, and the offspring of your body like the grains of sand..."

Now, back to the Great Jubilee.

Today, as I am writing in 2017, many believe we are in one of those great Jubilee years, that 50th year.

Remember it was actually 1967 when the Jewish people recaptured Jerusalem as their own. Therefore, if that were true, then go back fifty years earlier to 1917 were the British General, Allenby, took Jerusalem from the Ottoman Turks. That adds some validity to this 50-year Jubilee.

As I am writing this book, it is Yom Kippur (New Year), 5777 according to the Jewish calendar. This would be October 11, 2016 to 2017, according to the Roman calendar. This could put us in that great Jubilee year right now.

There was a Rabbi who lived in Germany, named Judah Ben Samuel who died in 1217 AD.

He wrote about this 50-year Jubilee. In it, he wrote, "When the Ottomans conquer Jerusalem, they will rule over Jerusalem for eight Jubilees. Afterwards, Jerusalem will become no-man's land for one Jubilee, and then in the ninth Jubilee it will once again come back into the possession of the Jewish nation – which would signify the beginning of the Messianic end time."

His words are not in the Bible so we should be very careful with this. That being said, it seems to be an accurate prediction.

The Ottomans did in fact conquer Jerusalem in 1517. They did rule over it for 8 Jubilees, which is 400 years, all the way to 1917.

After the British General defeated the Ottoman Turks in World War II, Jerusalem was a "No man's land". It was 50 years from 1917 to 1967 and during that time, no one had ownership of Jerusalem, not the Jews nor the Muslims.

Then he wrote that this ninth Jubilee, which so happens to be 1967, would be the Jubilee where Jerusalem would come back into the possession of the Jewish Nation. That has happened exactly in 1967. Israel took control of their ancient city after the six-day war of 1967.

Then he wrote that this would signify the beginning of the Messianic end time.

The end of times?

Notice he did not say the day or the hour. Jesus plainly said, "No one knows the day or the hour."

Jesus did say that we should know the seasons, and if we can understand the weather, we should know the times.

Remember Isaac Newton? He was a Christian genius who lived during the 1700's. He was a scientist who also was a Bible scholar. He wrote a commentary on Daniel. In it, he wrote that the 49 years in Daniel meant that when Jerusalem was restored to the Jewish people; add 49 years and this would signify the end of times.

This Great Jubilee stuff is interesting to look at as well as Isaac Newton's commentary. People of Isaac's day thought he was crazy to come up with this stuff but today it does not seem so far off.

Today, in our time, it appears we are in the last days. Our times seem to be a convergence zone of all of the signs that are shown to us in the Bible.

Israel is alive as a nation again and this is a huge sign.

Jesus said it would be like the days of Noah.

What was that like?

It was like Genesis chapter six, the time of Noah, where God said, "The earth also was corrupt before God, and the earth was filled with violence."

Hmm, sounds a lot like today's world. Corruption is at an all-time high, and violence is at a level never seen before.

Jesus said, "There will be wars and rumors of war". Sounds like today, does it not?

Jesus also said it would be as it was in the days of Lot.

What was that like?

It was the culture of Sodom and Gomora. Jesus also said, "They ate, they drank, they bought, they sold, they planted, they built." Those cities were doing well economically but they were also all about homosexuality. The cities of the world have turned toward this today.

These are huge signs. They are just like, "Red skies in the morning, sailor take warning."

Israel is a Nation again after over 2000 years.

The world as a whole is against Israel.

Israel has control of Jerusalem.

Jesus said, there would be earthquakes, famines, and pestilences. We have seen an increase in all of these.

Russia and Iran (Persia) are now allies for the first time in history. Ezekiel prophesied that this would happen in the latter times. He also wrote that they would come down against Israel.

The Jewish people are ready to build the third Temple.

Knowledge has increased greatly, just as Daniel wrote that it would in the later days.

We are seeing a huge push for a "One World Government", with a "New World Order". This stuff is not made up; our politicians use these words today.

Again, violence has increased throughout the world. Not the kind of violence we saw in World War I, and II, but this is different. This is violence toward the baby in the womb, family violence, community violence, racial violence, school violence, workplace violence. I believe this kind of corruption and violence has not been seen since the days of Noah.

All of these signs converge and point to this generation. However, God has a plan and has given us great hope.

Our great hope is Jesus Christ.

He is the Holy One who ascended into heaven.

Proverbs 30, gives us more:

"Who has ascended into heaven, or descended? Who has gathered the wind in His fists? Who has bound the waters in a garment? Who has established all the ends of the earth? What is His name, and what is His Son's name, if you know?"

We do know His wonderful name!

His great name is Jesus!

Jesus the Great.

Just look at His names in the Bible:

The Good Shepherd.

The Door for His sheep.

The Way.

The Truth.

The Life.

The First and the Last.

The Beginning and the End.

The Son of God.

Wonderful.

Counselor.

Mighty God.

Everlasting King.

King of King's.

Lord of Lord's.

Prince of Peace.

The Bright and Morning Star.

The Light of the World.

Ancient of Days.

The Great I Am.

The Bread from Heaven.

The Bread of life.

And...dare I say, "Tola'at Shani the Great".

Wow! How awesome are His names?

Now look at this beautiful, poetic scripture about the Lords return to rule the world seen in Psalm 96:

"Say among the nations, "The LORD reigns; The world also is firmly established, it shall not be moved; He shall judge the peoples righteously."

Let the heavens rejoice, and let the earth be glad; Let the sea roar, and all its fullness; Let the field be joyful, and all that is in it. Then all the trees of the woods will rejoice before the LORD.

For He is coming, for He is coming to judge the earth. He shall judge the world with righteousness, And the peoples with His truth."

What a beautiful scripture? *"Then the trees of the woods will rejoice before the LORD."*

One late summer afternoon, in the cool of the day, a light breeze was flowing. I was walking and praying to the Lord, when I saw some tall cottonwood trees moved by the wind.

They appeared to be swaying back and forth in worship of their creator. The leaves seemed to be clapping just like hands and even made the same sound. As they appeared to clap by the wind, they shimmered and reflected the sunlight like sparkling riffle water in a mountain stream. Then when I was passing underneath the shade, the sound was just like that of rushing water like a river.

Remember our fictional character from an earlier chapter named Ben?

Well, he was there at the cross, and saw Jesus cry out, "My God, My God why have you forsaken Me?"

Jesus' words moved Ben's heart. He knew it was the opening words to the Messianic Psalm 22. He started to quote out loud, "But I am a worm (Tola'at Shani) and no man".

Ben knew that prophecy of the Messiah was being fulfilled right before his eyes.

Ben had been a believer in Jesus from that day forward. He was a man filled by the Holy Spirit, on that day of Pentecost, 50 days after Jesus' resurrection. He had a heart for sharing the good news, and many came to know the Lord because Ben told them all about Jesus. He was a new man, living in Christ, and Christ living in him.

Ben was by no means a perfect man because he still sinned. Still a sinner but those sins are all nailed to the cross. The sins he did, the sins he struggled with at present time, and the sins he was going commit in the future were all nailed to that tree. All of it was covered by the blood of Jesus.

That tree, or cross, is just like the tree with the Tola'at Shani. The Tola'at Shani stuck itself to the tree, just as Jesus stuck himself to the cross. As the Tola'at Shani suffered death, its crimson red body was covering all of its offspring. The Tola'at Shani was providing life, a new birth to all of its own children.

Ben reflected that he was a changed man. He may have fell into sin a few times in his new life, but he always felt bad after he sinned, and he agreed with the conviction he felt in his heart. He would confess, and agree with God that what he did was a sin and then he would agree that he was forgiven. This gave him freedom.

Now imagine it was 30 to 40 years later, Ben died from old age. He died with a smile on his face because the peace of Jesus was in his soul. As he passed away, his loved ones wept, as they knew they were losing a loving man of God.

He truly was passing away. The air of this world became like liquid, it was as if he was emerging out of cloudy water and into the fresh blue sky. He emerged into the everlasting world where everything became so clear and the air so sweet.

When he left his body, he felt no pain. Then he heard music that caused his heart to warm with radiant burning of joy and gladness.

The great light was like the sparkle of the sun on the shimmering sea of emerald blue water. Ben knew as he moved closer, that the bright, beautiful light was the Lord Jesus Himself.

As he moved ever closer, he was walking through a sunny meadow which was covered with tiny bright blue flowers much like wooly thyme. As he walked on, the thyme was pleasantly crushed under his feet and the aroma was a sweet smelling mist. It filled the air like the fresh fragrance of lavender and honey.

As he drew close to Jesus, his heart and soul filled with the warmness of love and the air was pure and sweet, like a vineyard of sweet grapes in fresh mountain air.

As he drew near, there was a beautiful cobble stone rock wall no higher than his knees. Jesus was at the Gate, because He is the Good Shepherd and the Way for His sheep.

Ben knew this was the entrance into the Kingdom of Heaven and everything inside of him wanted to be there, with Jesus. This was home, and he was homesick for Heaven.

The Spirit of God filled the air around Ben. Then he breathed in and his heart smiled and sparkled with warm joy. He was so glad that the great light was none other than Jesus Himself. As he moved closer to Jesus, he was embraced by Him.

"Dear Lord Jesus. Thank you Lord." Ben said it with a great smile.

Then Jesus replied with a bright smile, "You, my friend, are welcome here. Welcome home Ben, come and enter into the Kingdom of God. You did well. You believed in Me, and followed Me. I remember well, that day when you first believed, when you saw what I did on that cross. I am so glad for you My friend," Ben heard this and wept with Joy and gladness.

Then Ben smelled the warm aroma of fresh baked bread. This bread smelled so, so good. At the same time, he heard the sound of rushing water pouring out, and into a cup. It too, smelled so sweet, so, good like the sweetest, richest wine since Jesus made it at the wedding in Cana, of Galilee.

Then Jesus said, "Come, eat freely of this bread of Heaven, and drink of the fruit of the vine."

As Ben ate and drank, he started to talk about how he remembered the Tola'at Shani. He shared how he knew the little Tola'at Shani was a tiny creature showing a great picture of the Lord.

Then he remembered a Proverb that brought all of this to light. He knew this was all about Jesus:

Wisdom has built her house, she has hewn out her seven pillars; She has slaughtered her meat, she has mixed her wine, she has also furnished her table. She has sent out her maidens, she cries out from the highest places of the city,

"Whoever is simple, let him turn in here!" As for him who lacks understanding, she says to him,

"Come, eat of my bread, and drink of the wine I have mixed."

Ben ate the bread, and drank the wine and was surrounded by his family and friends. Joy filled his whole being, from head to toe.

This was a setting like a café in the beautiful streets of Venice, but much better. Therefore, they all celebrated and danced together to the great music of Heaven. Ben heard stringed instruments, trumpets, flutes, drums, and voices singing praises to God the Father, God the Son, and God the Holy Spirit. Then his family and friends hugged him and smiled with him, as gladness seemed to overflow out of all of their hearts.

Perhaps our fictional story gives just a sneak preview of the true story of what we believers in Jesus will experience when we die.

Isaiah 55 Shows this well:

"Ho! Everyone who thirsts,
Come to the waters;
And you who have no money,
Come, buy and eat.
Yes, come, buy wine and milk

Without money and without price.
Why do you spend money for what is not bread,
And your wages for what does not satisfy?
Listen carefully to Me, and eat what is good,
And let your soul delight itself in abundance.
Incline your ear, and come to Me.
Hear, and your soul shall live;
And I will make an everlasting covenant with you—
The sure mercies of David.
Indeed I have given him as a witness to the people,
A leader and commander for the people.
Surely you shall call a nation you do not know,
And nations who do not know you shall run to you,
Because of the LORD your God,
And the Holy One of Israel;
For He has glorified you."
Seek the LORD while He may be found,
Call upon Him while He is near.
Let the wicked forsake his way,
And the unrighteous man his thoughts;
Let him return to the LORD,
And He will have mercy on him;
And to our God,
For He will abundantly pardon.
"For My thoughts are not your thoughts,
Nor are your ways My ways," says the LORD.
"For as the heavens are higher than the earth,
So are My ways higher than your ways,
And My thoughts than your thoughts.
"For as the rain comes down, and the snow from heaven,
And do not return there,
But water the earth,

And make it bring forth and bud,
That it may give seed to the sower
And bread to the eater,
So shall My word be that goes forth from My mouth;
It shall not return to Me void,
But it shall accomplish what I please,
And it shall prosper in the thing for which I sent it.
"For you shall go out with joy,
And be led out with peace;
The mountains and the hills
Shall break forth into singing before you,
And all the trees of the field shall clap their hands.
Instead of the thorn shall come up the cypress tree,
And instead of the brier shall come up the myrtle tree;
And it shall be to the LORD for a name,
For an everlasting sign that shall not be cut off."
Do you want to be there?

It's amazing how we work hard to make investments so that our retirement will be good. We act as though that is the ultimate goal in life, but at the same time, we ignore where our soul will retire forever. Heaven is for real, and Hell is for real. These are two real places, and they are places of forever, and ever, and ever, and ever...

If you want to go to Heaven, you must choose Jesus Christ, because He is the investment of eternity. You must believe in Him and be born again.

Are you invested in Jesus, or are you invested in the Ponzi scheme of Hell?

Even though we have no heavenly money to invest, the beautiful thing is, all he wants is you. He wants your heart to be His, and His to be yours.

This will start by believing in Jesus as your Lord and savior.

Proverbs 8 shows this well, *"I love those who love Me, and those who seek Me diligently will find Me. Riches and honor are with Me, enduring riches and righteousness. My fruit is better than gold, yes, than fine gold, and My revenue than choice silver."*

This is His amazing grace! Paul penned it well, *"For by grace you have been saved though faith, and that not of yourselves; it is the gift of God, not of works, lest anyone should boast."*

We will never be able to pay for our sins. Therefore, God invites us to go to His Son Jesus, who paid for it all, all of our sins. If we allow Him, He will wash us clean from the inside. There is a beautiful old hymn that was written based on the scripture of Isaiah 1:18.

"Jesus Paid it All".

It was composed in 1865, by Elvina M. Hall. Take a look:

I hear the Savior say,
"Thy strength indeed is small;
Child of weakness, watch and pray,
Find in Me thine all in all."
Jesus paid it all,
All to Him I owe;
Sin had left a crimson stain,
He washed it white as snow.
For nothing good have I
Whereby Thy grace to claim;
I'll wash my garments white
In the blood of Calv'ry's Lamb.
And now complete in Him,
My robe, His righteousness,
Close sheltered 'neath His side,
I am divinely blest.
Lord, now indeed I find
Thy pow'r, and Thine alone,

Can change the leper's spots
And melt the heart of stone.
When from my dying bed
My ransomed soul shall rise,
"Jesus died my soul to save,"
Shall rend the vaulted skies.

And when before the throne
I stand in Him complete,
I'll lay my trophies down,
All down at Jesus' feet.
Jesus paid it all.

Psalm 22 started with Jesus' same words from the cross, "My God, My God, why have You forsaken Me?"

Then the Psalm ended with, "Asah" (Hebrew), "Tetelestai" (Greek), the same words Jesus ended while on the cross, "It is finished", or "Paid in full".

Why not have a Jubilee now? You can be set free and guaranteed entrance into Heaven. It was paid in full for you, all you have to do is ask Jesus to forgive you of your sins, and ask Him to be your Lord and Savior.

He would love to see you in Heaven, just like our character Ben. Just come to the foot of that tree, the cross of Calvary, and believe just as Ben believed. Let your crimson stain be covered on that cross just like the red stain of the Tola'at Shani, then it will turn as white as snow.

Jesus is ready to forgive you of all of your sins. "The blood of Jesus Christ His Son cleanses us from all sin" (First John 1:7).

ABOUT THE AUTHOR

George was born in Santa Cruz, California and raised by a loving mother and father who are followers Jesus. They taught him the Bible from his earliest years. He was raised in a large ministry that helped people right off of the street with drug problems. His family became an outreach in Albuquerque, New Mexico in 1979. He was 9 years old when they moved there and was starting to get into a lot of trouble.

He attended Calvary Albuquerque when it started in 1982. It was during that time that "Seeds" were being planted in his heart by hearing the Word of God taught by Pastor Skip Heitzig.

It was a year later in Tucson, Arizona that he gave his life to Jesus and was "Born Again".

His family moved back to Santa Cruz when he was 14 and he became an avid surfer. Surfing became his life and slowly he drifted away from close relationship with Jesus.

At twenty-one years old, he knew that living to surf was a dead end. Therefore, he volunteered to become an Army Ranger. During this time in the Rangers, he learned how to be a man. Though he learned much, he was still a lost son to God. The party life was everything until he met the love of his life, Christina. Later they married and they moved back to his home town of Santa Cruz.

His wife, work and surfing was his priority until they had their first child in 2002. Later they decided that it would be better to raise their son in Washington State. He started to go to church again and turn back toward the Lord.

It was at a men's conference at Calvary Fellowship in Seattle that he re-committed his life to Jesus. Greg Laurie was preaching and he felt the touch in his heart of the Holy Spirit to stand up for the prayer of re-dedication to Jesus.

Since that time, he began to teach and preach at his Church and many of these Sunday sermons and Wednesday night teachings became books as well.

Don't miss out!

Visit the website below and you can sign up to receive emails whenever George Crabb publishes a new book. There's no charge and no obligation.

https://books2read.com/r/B-A-XHIEB-VEKYC

BOOKS2READ

Connecting independent readers to independent writers.

Also by George Crabb

Jesus in the Old Testament
Tola'at Shani - The Crimson Worm of Psalm 22

Standalone
Ani Yosef
Road to Emmaus
The Same Today
See Jesus in the Old Testament

Watch for more at www.georgecrabb.com.

About the Author

I'm George Crabb, author and bible teacher who has served in ministry for over 25 years in the local church and I have a heavy burden on my heart to get holistic and true Bible teaching and knowledge of Jesus into the lives of others.

Read more at https://www.georgecrabb.com/.